Important Note

Introduction

Effective Management

Managing by Values

The Manager's Role

What is Your Management Style?

Managing Performance

Summary

Attachments

Managing Employees Series

Copyright

Important Note

I hope this book *Performance Management: Coach, Counsel, or Terminate* helps you increase your effectiveness as a manager and the performance of your employees. This book is not a comprehensive guide to engaging employees and handling performance in the work-place. This guide highlights tools to use to increase the performance of your teams.

It is important to be aware of the federal and state employment laws as well as any contractual agreements the company may have with the employee. For specific advice geared to an issue, consult an expert. No book or other published material is a substitute for personalized advice from a knowledgeable lawyer who practices employment law in your state.

Pat Brill

Introduction

In every industry, in every service field, businesses deal with people, whether it's customers, partners, competitors, suppliers, or technicians. No matter who they are or what their relationship is to your business, the way you and your employees interact with outsiders is indicative of how well you run your business. Whether you realize it or not, a significant amount of your sales depends upon your employee's active and productive performance during hours of operation.

Not only do you need to be aware of each employee's behavior with external connections, but it's equally important to ensure that employees have positive and respectful ways to interact with other employees. Respectful behavior helps employees build trust with each other, creates a more collaborative work environment and ultimately impacts the relationship with customers.

Unfortunately, work is also one of the most stressful aspects of modern life. Even your best employees – and you – will have learning curves to master, and will deal with difficult or 'bad' days, which will consume a lot of your time.

Managing employees is time-consuming, so consider how you want to use your time best to engage your team members and meet your business goals.

To effectively manage employees, it takes skill and a solid understanding of how to best work with each member of your team. If you are the new manager, you will have the additional challenge of changing roles from a peer to a manager.

Before you can do that, step back and become aware of your current style of interaction with others in the organization. You can only do what you know, so missing management skills makes it challenging to lead your team as well as set the foundation in place for high performance.

You can learn how to be an effective manager.

Effective Management

A broad definition of effective management would be the ability to motivate your teams to perform at a high level to meet business goals consistently. Is that the only evaluation point? What about ngaged employees? What about motivating employees to be their best and encouraging them to develop more knowledge and skills? At the end of the day, no matter what style a manager has in their toolbox, the role is to achieve the business goals and lead their team members.

How do you incorporate the various moving parts in managing employees? There are necessary components of effective management: communication, accountability, conflict management, and employee recognition.

Communication

Communication, just like in all relationships, is the foundation for effective management. Used mindfully, you can provide clear, concise, and consistent information to your employees. When you have created your message, it's important to be aware of your receiver. Otherwise, the meaning may be diluted or not received at all.

Communication comes in different methods: face-to-face, meetings, email, phone, training, Skype, or word of mouth. Naturally, word-of-mouth can weaken the information and potentially cause the most problems.

Managers have different communication skills, and this will impact the effectiveness of their interactions with their team members. Each person has their way of leading teams. Their style may work well with some employees and hinder a working relationship with another. Again, it's important to be aware of the receiver and how he or she may take in information. For example, if you want to make an employee aware of his or her performance, do it in private when you can maintain a positive approach regarding the change.

Managers use several different communication styles depending on the situation, the person, or their emotional levels. They came to these methods usually by emulating managers they had in the past, watching others, considering their comfort levels in interacting with others, and adding other learning points to their management style.

Accountability

Wouldn't it be great if your employees do what they are supposed to do, and more? Employees have distinct levels of accountability skills, and in managing employees, you need to help them to maximize this competence. Some employees need minimum direction to execute their work. Others get distracted, and at the end of the day, they were busy, but not necessarily productive.

Accountability is about taking responsibility and following through to completion on your commitments. To effectively manage employees, you need to know how to keep them accountable.

You are responsible for keeping your employees accountable, and your staff is accountable for getting the work done.

The question then is how can you help build your employee's "accountability muscles?"

3 Basic Steps to Create Employee Accountability

<u>Create Clear Priorities</u>

I've have heard from many employees how management keeps changing directions. They complain that there are too many projects going on at the same time. It's important to be clear about company goals, communicate the priorities to each employee and ensure they are accountable for their work.

In managing employees, what is your priority? You will get the most from your employees when you are clear about the goals and how each of your team members contributes to the success of the department or company. Take the time to create your master plan and share this with everyone on your team.

Present the information in different formats:

- Department meeting
- Share the plan documents
- Follow up emails
- 1:1 meeting with each of your team members

Clarity around priorities helps you and your employees.

Set Clear Expectations

Now that you have created your master plan and have communicated your plan to each member of your team, it's time for you to work with your employees.

What type of manager are you? Do you micromanage your employees, do you take a hands-off approach with them, or do you set clear goals and expectations and then let them deliver? Too many managers micro manage, overreact, or have a 'hands off' approach. Neither style will build 'accountability' within your organization.

Your focus is to establish a balance between setting goals, creating performance expectations, and creating follow-up meetings to ensure accountability.

What if an employee doesn't meet expectations? It's important for you to be clear about the consequences for non-performance. Have an intervention process in place that will help you support your employees. Be diligent in following up with employee's performance levels. Consistent and clear communication with each person helps minimize performance issues. Be there with them -- coaching them to be their best.

If you provide coaching and counseling and the employee is still not performing, you need to take quick action for yourself, the employee, and the rest of the team. Learn more about handling low performance or negative attitudes that are not productive for the well-being of your team.

Be consistent in handling your team members. Your employees will respond favorably when a manager is fair and respectful to all.

Be Accountable Yourself

A significant impact on your employee's performance is the strength of your 'accountability muscles.' Do you follow through on what you say you will do? Are you available to listen to your staff? Your team will follow you if they feel you respect them. They will emulate your behavior and actions. Take the time to create your 3-step process:

- Identify your employee management priorities.
- Identify the expectations you have for yourself.

- Evaluate your accountability.

Be known as an active accountability manager, and your team will respond accordingly.

Quick Point

Focus your attention on the three priorities in developing 'accountability muscles' within your team – create clear priorities, set clear expectations, and be accountable yourself. If accountability is not becoming stronger with

every team member, start back at priority number 1 – create clear priorities. Then go through each step until you have mastered your ability to be a strong accountability manager.

Conflict Management

Conflict occurs when there is a difference between two or more people, when the emotions are heightening, and resolution is breaking down. Conflict occurs with a manager and employee or between team members. Differences between team members can be useful as it offers more input into a situation which can provide stronger projects and team relationships. Different perspectives can enhance the growth of the team members and increase the success of a project. It creates energy and engagement of team members.

Where it becomes a conflict is when there is no resolution in place, and the people have broken the bond, and no one is willing to collaborate to create a solution. If your team members can't find a solution to the issue, you will need to facilitate the solution with their participation. The workplace can become toxic if the manager doesn't step in to help team members resolve their issues.

Conflict in the workplace is inevitable in that people working together eight hours each day will not agree with each other, will find certain styles of communication to be offensive, will feel someone doesn't listen to them and will have different perspectives than others. All this can happen in one day.

Being knowledgeable with conflict resolution is important. Conflict happens in organizations, and finding the balance between conflict that creates energy and conflict that breaks down is where you need to focus your attention. It's part of coaching your team members.

To effectively manage conflict resolution with your team members:

Catch the Conflict Early

As soon as you are aware of the conflict, handle it. Small conflicts are manageable. A significant conflict with a long history behind it is harder to resolve. For example, if an employee's communication style is hindering the well-being of your team, then make the employee aware of what he or she is doing and how it is creating conflict within the team. Another example, two employees sit next to each other. Some employees talk out loud when they work. It's a habit they have, though it creates a distraction for the employee who sits next to them.

Don't avoid the conflict because it seems minor. It's a perfect time to help an employee become more mindful of his or her performance or behavior. It's also a perfect time to teach employees how to resolve small conflicts while they are manageable.

Yes, people have their quirks, and you don't want to make everyone the same. But be aware when quirks are impacting the performance of the individual as well as the team.

Keep in mind that employees watch what you do. If you have a tough time handling conflict, they will lose trust in you. You need to quickly act when handling issues that impact your team.

Listen Carefully

You may make assumptions around individual's performance or behavior without taking the time to listen thoroughly, which can exacerbate the issue. Conflict management is about gathering the information, allowing people to express their views, and have them help define the problem.

Be mindful of people and situations around you. When working within a conflict zone, be sure to take deep breaths. Be aware of your thoughts or any preconceived ideas surrounding the issue(s). By being aware, you can release unnecessary tensions before dealing with conflicts and provide more room for you to step back and listen.

Don't look for right or wrong, rather find solutions that help both people feel heard with a reasonable solution for both parties.

Find common ideas where the parties can agree; this will create a solid foundation.

Create ways for everyone to brainstorm potential solutions and then come to an agreement as to what actions will work for everyone.

Schedule a follow-up time with the parties to evaluate whether the solution handled the issue or if there are open problems that still exist. Conflict management isn't a perfect 1-2-3 solution; rather it's consistent follow up to ensure the individuals are working on the solutions.

Employees are people with perceptions and beliefs, and no matter what you do to help them, they may go back to the original conflict and continue to escalate their annoyances. What can you do then? It's when the disciplinary action comes into play. When employees don't deal with their performance or change their behaviors, it impacts the team and the overall success of the company.

Prevent Conflict

One of the best ways to avoid conflict is to create clear guidelines for appropriate behavior in the workplace.

- Stress the importance of everyone being accountable for his or her performance and actions. Be clear about what accountability looks like so they can emulate it.

- Create a basic rule that there is zero tolerance for disrespect towards others. Disrespect shows up in the workplace through criticizing ideas, a manager yelling at an employee, being sarcastic with a coworker, making jokes about the person behind his or her back and several other behaviors that devalue an employee.

- In the U.S. some laws protect employees from discrimination or sexual harassment. As a manager, you need to be aware of the laws and the legal ramification when you or an employee breaks them. For example, in your role as a manager, you are in the lunchroom, and you hear an employee making fun of an employee because of their race, color, religion, or sex. Your responsibility is to handle that issue immediately. If the individual is not your direct report, go to the manager of that person and have the employee come to discuss the issue. Train your employees on the laws, and don't assume they know.

- Lots of people are uncomfortable dealing with conflicts, and you need to guide them in recognizing the issues, and that it may be their response to the problem that could be causing the conflict. They will need to be active in resolving the issue. Even if they are willing to work through issues, you may still need to facilitate appropriate solutions to their problems.

Let employees know that you are there to work with them as they deal with any workplace issues that interfere with their performance. It's their job to resolve it, and you are there to facilitate the resolution.

If you are the only one who comes up with recommendations, then your employees will never take ownership of their problems. Encourage them to be open to finding potential solutions.

Encourage them to share amongst themselves how they have resolved conflicts as this helps others, as well as reduces your need to facilitate conflicts within your team.

How a manager handles conflict also impacts how the team deals with its conflicts.

Quick Point

Keep in mind the three ways you can master conflict management: catch the conflict early, listen carefully and prevent conflict.

Managing by Values

What are Values?

Values are beliefs or ideals that influence behaviors on how a person acts in different situations. They are typically stable and express themselves in how you live and work.

When managing your team, become mindful around your behaviors as it indicates to your employees what you value. Also, listen to what is important to your team members as they are expressing their values.

The clearer you are about the values that are important to you, the more satisfied you will be with yourself and your relationships with others. When you live by your values, you increase your self-respect, set clear guidelines around what is important to you, easier to make decisions, help clarify and keep your team members focused and finally you enjoy your life better.

Some core values can help you in business: accountability, celebrations, excellence, creativity, family, diversity, learning, honesty, integrity, respect or service.

Honesty and integrity are high values that build a foundation of trust with your employees. These values are also part of accountability, and if you focus on them for yourself and your team, you will most likely have a successful high-performing team.

Take some time to do your research and go online to see an extended list of values and select your top five values. When you review them, think about a time when you felt most happy or satisfied because embedded in those times are values that produced those good feelings. Then put them in order 1 to 5 and work on creating a professional and personal life that supports your values.

> **Quick Point**
> Create your top 5 values and define why they are important to you. Include in that statement how you will keep those values in front of you when working with your employees.

Why are Values Important?

Values guide you in your decision-making process, whether you are aware of them or not. You build a life around your values. For example, if being physically healthy is important to you and you work eighty hours a week with no time to work out, then you will feel internal stress. Your values are not in balance.

In managing employees, if your stated value is to show respect to all your team members, and you consistently cancel meetings with them, then you are out of balance in your work life.

Values are personal guides that allow you to grow, do your best, be respectful to others, and build a life that offers personal and professional satisfaction.

Your Vision of Management

All companies require a strong vision statement to market their products or services. It is a tool for employees to integrate the company's vision in all that they do. This vision will need to be part your management.

A vision is a statement about "where you want to be." It's evaluating where you are now and where you see yourself in the future. Align our management style with the company's vision.

Your organization's purpose, values, and culture create the environment that will affect every employee. What are your organization's purpose, values, and culture? For example, if one of the company's values is quality, how is it incorporated into the culture of the organization?

- How do you embody the vision of the business in managing your teams?
- How do you keep the vision in front of your employees?
- How do you encourage improvement in performance to meet the vision?

Create Your Vision

The importance of vision is to focus attention on what matters and what type of manager do you want to be.

Take the time to create your vision of your management style that supports the company and inspires your team to perform at its best. In building this vision, think of effective ways to encourage others to support the vision of the company.

Focus on Your Vision

It's not easy to always be aware of your vision, though if you create reminders and stay focused on the essential ingredients of managing people, you will ultimately find you are more productive in your management style.

You will share this vision in all that you do, and others on your team will respond accordingly and be more engaged and involved in the success of the business.

The Manager's Role

When it comes to performance improvement, the role of the manager is an important thing to understand. As the title suggests, the manager's job is to manage just about every aspect of a company. That said, you don't have enough time to investigate and follow up on all the minute details of your business; you can delegate a lot of the work, but you are still primarily responsible for what goes on.

Dealing with behavioral and performance issues is an essential core function of your role. Using coaching and counseling skills are essential tools to handle the daily matters that surface.

> **Quick Point**
>
> If you are diligent in handling issues while small, you will be able to prevent larger issues.

When there is a problem with one of your employees (provided it is not a serious one), you can start investigating the root of the problem for yourself. Spend time getting all the facts about a situation before passing judgment. It is your role to lead your team to robust solutions.

For example, if an employee displays negative behavior, there are a couple of questions you might ask them before you refer to your performance plan and decide on a course of action to correct the problem.

1) Is something bothering them? Is there a personal issue or a work-related issue that has recently upset them?

2) Are they under an unusual amount of pressure? If so, would it help to talk about it with someone?

3) Are they getting enough sleep?

Step back and come up with your questions to help you and the employee address performance or behavior issues. Check in with your employees for their input as well. If an employee has consistently underperformed, it's time to find out what is causing the issue.

A few other questions to consider are:

1) Are current performance expectations unreasonable? If so, what expectations would be more reasonable?

2) Is the employee struggling to perform because he or she doesn't feel competent with their responsibilities? If so, what is lacking? Would additional training help to boost their confidence and productivity?

Your job as a manager is to look after the health of your business.

Talking with your employees and taking a general interest in their well-being builds a healthy work relationship. During work hours, your employees are your responsibility, and the more transparent your communication is with them, the better they are likely to perform and feel part of a valued team.

Manager's Responsibility

As a manager, you are there to inform employees what each position requires and to give them the opportunity to meet those requirements and expectations. I know that you have heard this before; you may not realize just how critical your role is to the bottom line of the company's profits. If you build and implement strong management skills, your staff, as well as the company, will thrive in a very competitive business environment.

How do you become a manager capable of leading a team? Focus on ensuring that your staff is successful. *Most employees will perform at or above standards.* Some will not. When you recognize that an employee's performance or behavior is not as expected, take the time to address the issues.

When you engage employees quickly around performance or behavior issues, you give them the opportunity to resolve problems, move forward, and feel more competent. Find a quiet time in the day and week to meet with the employee and have a casual and general discussion about the issue with performance or behavior. Let them know it's an open discussion between the two of you to understand what is creating the work issue.

Managers can find it difficult to speak with an employee, especially if you have any of the following concerns:

- that the employee may react defensively;

- that the current labor market is tight; or

- that the issue seems minor and mentioning it could de-motivate your employee

---

Quick Point

Remember: providing employees with appropriate and timely feedback can be a positive experience for everyone.

Employees usually want to correct their behavior. You can guide them by:

- informing them what the problem is and what they must do to fix it

- establishing a reasonable period to fix the problem

- letting your employee know the consequences of not fixing the problem

- asking them what you can do to assist them in this process

By communicating your expectations clearly to all team members, you set the standards for performance and behavior. Not every employee will measure up to performance standards, and when this occurs, you need to take the necessary steps to help them correct the problem.

Listening

Listening is a critical skill to managing a team, and often neglected by managers. A manager has a lot on their plates and often listen partially and don't get all the information nor stop to understand the employee. With partial information or previous experiences with the employee, a manager's decision probably won't be the best one.

If a manager is known not to listen, employees will feel less motivated or engaged in their work. Employees are people, and they need to feel respected for who they are, how they can contribute to the success of the company, and providing supportive feedback on their performance.

Studies show that one of the most prominent reasons an employee leaves is because of their manager. You are responsible for building a strong working environment, so you need to build your listening skills to provide the best coaching and tools for each person.

> **Quick Point**
>
> Active listening gains the employee's trust. You show you care for them, and they, in turn, will provide you with the same confidence and attention.

Equal to building strong working relationships with employees, when a manager listens, they also receive valuable business information that will help them manage projects or anticipate potential business issues. Employees have information a manager can use to be successful in their business.

It's important to have a mindfulness practice as it helps you build "listening muscles." Let go of the past; don't think about all you need to do in the future, and instead stay present with the person. Mindfulness doesn't mean that you have to spend hours listening; rather you can say to the person, "I only have ten minutes right now, or we can speak later at a better time." Most of the time, the employee requires a short amount of time but needs the full attention of the manager.

What are the benefits of listening while engaging with others?

- You shut down your thoughts and listen to the other person. Listening minimizes the time that you are in reaction mode by not giving your full attention to the facts. When you listen, you are available to receive more information, which guides you in making decisions.

- As you listen, you can ask questions to gather further understanding. Questions ensure that the employee is clear about the information.

- Listening allows you to build stronger working relationships with your team members. They feel you respect them when you take the time to listen to them. Employees who feel heard to are usually loyal to their manager and are more engaged in their work.

- While you are listening to the employee, listen to your thoughts to see whether you have enough room to hear what he or she has to say. If you are pretending to listen, while figuring out what to say next, the employee will know and not feel heard. You are just wasting your time.

- When an employee feels listened to, he or she is more open to listening to you.

If you think your listening skills are not that strong, what can you do to improve them?

- Practice giving your full attention by eliminating distractions. For example, mute your phone, shut down your email, and even move away from your office to give your full attention.

- Always may eye contact with the speaker.

- Take deep breaths to clear your head, so you are available to listen.

- Allow the speaker some time to get their thoughts out. Again, if you have limited time, indicate so and schedule another time when you are available. Providing a time limit is okay. This way you feel more comfortable giving them your full attention because you both know there is a time limit.

- If you feel frustrated with an employee because he or she is rambling and not concise in their communication, you can provide feedback that you need them to be clearer in their thoughts.

- Ask questions or give them feedback on what you think they said. Sum up their thoughts for clarity.

Recognition

Employees need recognition, and the more you offer, the more they will respond. Companies may have a formal recognition program, though you, the manager, need to incorporate an informal recognition process into your regular interactions with your team members. The more immediate your appreciation, the most impact you will have continuing the performance or behaviors you want to encourage with your group.

Informal recognition ties to specific performance or behavior. For example:

- an employee who reaches out to help another person on the team

- the employee initiated a solution that helped the team

- the employee offered to stay late to get the project completed

Informal recognition is powerful because it is usually immediate, specific to the employee, and makes the employee feel appreciated. It's also good to have some money in the budget for simple recognition awards. Some quick and immediate recognition actions you can give to your team members are:

- A simple "thank you" works perfectly, indicating to the employee what they did and how it helped the team or project.

- A quick gift card or dinner on us after an employee worked hard to get work done.

- If your team is working hard, give them a break and bring in lunch. Provide time to relax, and this lets the team know you appreciate the hard work.

- If you hear positive feedback from someone else, let the employee know about it. You can create a weekly "recognition" email indicating each employee's contribution during the week.

- If you have the budget and team members have been working hard, give them gift cards to a dinner out for two.

If you want your employees to be fully engaged, then you need to reach out and let them know how much you appreciate their contributions to the project and other members of the team.

> **Quick Point**
> Everyone wants to be recognized, so find the best way to let each employee know he or she is important. Some people love group recognition, while others prefer a quiet 1:1 thank you. Know your team members.

Everyone knows that recognition is a powerful motivator. Though knowing that recognition is important and doing it are different animals. Where do you stand on the recognition scale from 1 to 10?

If you think you are active in this area, check in with your employees as they usually rate their managers lower.

Do you think you don't have time to stop and thank your employees? It's just good business sense to build the habit of recognizing your employees. Studies after studies have done the work for you as they have proven that consistent recognition increases productivity considerably -- time well spent.

The informal appreciation is not about company-wide programs, rather how you, the manager, can make a difference with your employees in your daily interactions. Managing employees is about motivating employees, and recognition is a powerful tool. Does it sound contrived to make a conscious effort to recognize a team member? It's never contrived, yet I do acknowledge that when we are changing a habit or learning something new, we are awkward. Recognizing your employees is just a habit, and they say it takes twenty-one days to change a habit. To increase your awareness and implementation of recognition, here are some thoughts for you.

- Even though you manage a team, the power of recognition lies at the individual employee level.

- Find out about them, what's important to them, and what they do for fun. If you provide a special thank you just for the individual, you will know what they like.

- Start the recognition right at the beginning – the new hire.

- Get out of the office and find opportunities to recognize individuals on work they are performing in the moment they are doing it. The only way you can build your "recognition habit" is by doing it.

- Keep a list of each employee and every time he/she takes the initiative, performs quality work, learns something new, or helps another teammate. Write it down. When you are in your 1:1 with this person, let them know.

- Take time to research ideas on recognition, so you have a stronger toolbox in motivating your employees.

Managing employees takes time and commitment on your part. Make a commitment to yourself to develop your knowledge and skills in recognizing your employees. Find one action you can do today and start doing it.

Disengaged Employees

Employees are critical to your business success. If you could do it all yourself, then you wouldn't need them. If you can't, then you need them fully engaged and doing their best. The studies indicate that more and more employees are not fully involved in their work and the percentage of disengaged employees is increasing each year. How do you know if they are disengaged?

- They start complaining more about the work environment, people in it, too much work, and other issues that surface up.

- They lack excitement and do just the minimum of what is needed.

- They make excuses why they couldn't get the work done.

- They show a lack of initiative.

- They no longer seem interested in learning.

Employees who are not engaged and do just what they need to do to complete the job is frustrating because they are doing the work but barely. So how do you elevate their performance levels?

You need to find out what disengaged them.

- If you believe they could do more, check in with them by asking how satisfied they are with their responsibilities.
- Ask them if your management style adds to their overall performance or decreases it. Studies show that employees leave their manager more than the company.
- Find out if the team is supportive and collaborative or disengages them.

What is Your Management Style?

Whether you are a new manager or one who has worked with employees for a long time, you still need to step back and view your management style. If you were interviewing for another management position, how would you evaluate your style? What attributes do you currently use in managing staff?

Before you can embark on incorporating the components, you need first to review the current management styles you rely on to motivate your employees to perform. A management style is considered a way of making decisions and interacting with team members. What has worked and not worked for you in creating a stable workplace for your employees?

There are several types of management styles.

Autocratic

This style of management was historically the primary way managers related to their staff. They would manage by controlling most aspects of the work and give little autonomy to the employees. This style of management is focused on tasks and not necessarily on people. The manager makes the decision without input from team members.

Without the employee's agreement to a decision, the manager has to work hard to keep them focused and productive.

Hands Off

The 'Hands Off' manager tends to stand back and provides limited direction which allows the employees to decide how to complete their work.

Hands off style work with highly skilled and knowledgeable employees who can move forward quickly with the work. This type of manager will provide guidance, though only when needed. The downside of this style is the manager is not aware what is required until there is a fire to put out, or until an employee's performance diminishes, or their behavior interferes with the other team members.

Being hands off doesn't mean a manager isn't empowering their employees, rather he or she is not actively managing.

Teamwork

Teamwork managers focus on collaboration and direct employees to create solutions and solve problems as a team. This style focuses on the relationships of each member of the team, as well as meeting the project or business deliverables.

A manager that builds a dedicated team with great talent and facilitates each person's contribution and growth will be successful in their business. Teamwork requires collaboration, and managers help employees handle conflicts within the team as well as provide clear direction for the team.

An active manager supports, coaches, facilitates conflict resolution and recognizes each team member.

Democratic

A democratic style of management allows employees to help build direction of a project through consensus. The employees participate in the decision-making process. Everyone provides ideas and can have input into the final decision.

The downside of this style is it could slow down the decision-making process. It's important for the manager to facilitate the discussions and then bring the information together to make the best decision.

Transactional

Transactional management is a highly structure leadership style that provides rewards and negative feedback to meet the desired results. For example, large corporations and military are organizations that embody this type of management style. These types of managers set high-performance standards for self and the group. Though this can be an effective management style, a potential downside is that the manager tells and micromanages the tasks to ensure success in meeting deadlines.

Transformational

A transformational manager is visible because he or she focuses on motivation and collaboration. He or she will work with employees to identify the change and create a vision to guide the change through motivation and inspiration.

Management by Walking Around

By walking around, this management style allows the manager to be aware of the level of morale, watch what employees are doing, ask questions around their current work, all with the concern to minimize potential issues. The downside to this style is employees may perceive that the manager is micromanaging, or taking too much responsibility for the work when listening to employees.

Chaotic

Chaotic management is an interesting style as it gives total control over decision-making process to employees. This type of style can create innovative ideas. The manager makes sure that the team members are fully engaged in their growth and the company's success.

Entrepreneur

An entrepreneurial manager isn't a manager, rather is a visionary. The plus of this style is the manager's energy. He or she is willing to help employees grow because there is so much to do. The employee has to be flexible as clear given the ongoing demand of starting a new company. A self-motivated employee fits well with this type of management style.

No one person is just one type of manager; rather most people have a blend of a couple of methods. Having said that, all managers tend to lean on one style in their daily operations. All styles have their strengths and weaknesses. When you recognize your most comfortable style, ask yourself:

Does your management style provide you with the best performance from your team?

Evaluate what is working and what is stopping your employees from doing their best. One way to is to get feedback. Ask your team members how you can best manage them. Each employee has diverse needs and knowing how you can best work with each person will make your job a lot easier, and your employee's performance will become stronger.

Unclear, Distracted Management

Managers are responsible for business deliverables as well as ensure the performance of their team members. In today's global business environments, goals rapidly change, and distracted management could potentially hinder a manager from focusing clearly on their goals.

Another aspect of distracted management is the manager's ability to focus on the multiple aspects of their responsibilities. Some people are more easily distracted than others which can hinder a person's ability to manage a project and team members. We all have traits that infringe on our effectiveness as a manager.

A typical day for a manager will include different technology and people interruptions. Some interruptions are necessary and need to be quickly dealt with and knowing how to manage other issues that are not critical requires full attention. Technology and people provide the biggest distractions for a manager, and it would be helpful if there is a plan in place to handle both of them at appropriate times in your day.

Quick Point

Step back and see how many unnecessary distractions you allow into your day that takes away from your top goals. No judgment, rather observe what stops you from being more efficient in your work day. Name the different distractions: email, people, meetings that are not critical to your immediate goals for the day.

What is Mindfulness?

Mindfulness is paying attention on purpose, accepting our thoughts and feelings without judgment and becoming aware what is happening around us.

Mindfulness has its roots in spiritual communities, though is integrated more in the business world as a tool to build strong work environments. It helps managers pay attention to what is occurring in the present and to make corrections that support team members and the business goals.

Why Is Mindfulness an Effective Management Style?

Mindfulness management is allowing yourself to stay focused on what needs to be done now to reach your business goals. It's being aware of all the different moving parts and selecting what is most important to move a project ahead in the right manner. It's about letting go of the past and not being anxious about the future, but rather stay focused in the moment.

Mindfulness management helps your employees reduce reactionary responses and increase their decision-making skills. The more closely aligned you are with your employees, the easier it is to coach them rather than have them in the performance improvement path.

It's slowing you down and thinking about where to put your focus best.

To create this type of management style, you will need to practice mindfulness.

As a manager, you set the direction of projects as well communicate to employees the priorities. If you are more aware of your feelings and thoughts, you can regulate and make changes within yourself that add more value to your relationships and ultimately to the success of your team.

Mindfulness Practice

To be effective as a manager, you require an awareness of your current management style. Then you need to decide what is the best management style for you. When you decide on a fresh style of management, there is always learning and uncomfortable feelings, and you may feel stilted in your efforts.

Choosing mindfulness management means you will also put aside time to sit quietly and practice being mindful. That is the only way you can set the foundation for being more in the present with yourself, employees, and the business. When you are present at the moment, no matter how stressful the situation seems, you and the employee are at the moment working together.

Decide to set aside each day at least twenty minutes to sit quietly with your thoughts. If sitting quietly for 20 minutes seems challenging in the beginning, set a goal for 5-10 minutes.

As you become more comfortable with the practice, you can add additional minutes to your quiet time. When you sit, release the expectations that you must have no thoughts while you practice.

You will have thoughts and moments of quiet as this is part of practicing mindfulness. The focus of mindfulness is to be aware of your thoughts. As you sit with your thoughts, you recognize you are thinking and allow the thoughts to move forward.

You can start your work day with this practice which will set the foundation of being present with your work, people, and decisions throughout the day.

You gently breathe in and out, allowing this quiet time to reduce the noise you carry around with you. How does this practice reduce the noise?

Like with any new endeavor, practice builds those "awareness muscles." Awareness of your thoughts, without judgment, provides you will have the opportunity to be present to what is occurring in the moment. This knowledge will give you greater clarity in your day-to-day situations.

When being mindful, you might be focusing on one's breath, breathing in and out. When a thought pops up, you can just acknowledge, "I am thinking." This acknowledgment doesn't attach itself to the thought but rather allows you the awareness that you are thinking.

Why is it important to create a mindfulness practice? The more you learn to be present with your thoughts, the more capable your ability to focus on what is important and what is just thoughts that pass through you.

You can use this new level of awareness to observe the performance of your team members. You let go of previous thoughts about who they are and instead become more aware of them and what they need to be their best.

Open Mind

Mindfulness creates an open mind. How does an open mind work in business? It creates a higher level of curiosity and receptivity to the people around you and new possibilities for you and your team members. It helps you to accept others, recognize their strengths, utilize their abilities and let go what no longer works. Change is part of life and being open by practicing mindfulness, will enhance your ability to deal with change.

*You can only do one thing at a time --
use mindfulness to be your best in the moment.*

Workplace Stress

If you have done your research, you will know that job-related stress is on the rise. The economy, global competition, gender gaps, long hours, layoffs, constant change in project focus, and 24/7 connection have all added to the overall ineffectiveness of employees. Managers are hiring less staff and increasing workloads of their existing employees to increase profit margins.

Employees who suffer from stress perform at lower levels and are the least engaged in the workplace. Not all stress is bad because employees who are working hard towards the completion of the project, ultimately feel good about themselves, and the heightened stress levels are only for a given period.

It's good to take the temperature of your stress levels and those of your team members. First, review the areas where you are feeling stressed. Is it caused by too much to do, demanding project timelines, or is it employee related where performance levels are not meeting the business goals? Some indicators that an employee is operating at high-stress levels:

- The employee is absent more often.
- Their behavior has changed. Maybe he or she is irritated or more remote in the daily interactions.
- They're not meeting their deadlines.
- Their work is sloppy.
- They're defensive.

If you are stressed, or a team member is struggling with their work responsibilities, then it's time to step back and reflect on the cause. Employees handle stress in different ways. Some people have a high threshold for it, and others feel the impact of stress almost immediately. Knowing an individual's threshold will help you better manage their reactions. You can do that in the way you communicate the information he or she needs to have.

For example, senior management is putting pressure on you to complete a project earlier than originally expected. Your team has been working hard to meet the original deadline, and now an earlier timetable will only add more pressure. How can you communicate to your team, to minimize reactionary mode and work in solution mode?

Work or personal issues can increase levels of stress. Sometimes an employee has a personal problem that is causing them stress, and this will impact their performance.

> **Quick Point**
>
> A practical monthly activity is to close out each month, reflecting on the areas which were stressful for either you and the individuals on the team. You cannot remove all stress, though checking in on a regular basis allows you to minimize the impact of stress.

Again, being mindful of what is occurring for you and your team will increase your employee's engagement and improve performance.

Your Management Strengths and Weaknesses

The above list of styles includes generalized descriptions of different management styles. It's good to step back now and evaluate where your style has been effective. For example, if you were responsible for a project, evaluate how effective were you in providing clear, concise, and consistent communication, so team members were aware of the whole project and how their work integrated with the rest of the team. What skills did you use to create that success?

How strong are your listening, accountability, communication or conflict management skills? These are core skills that enhance or distract employee's performance.

Managing Performance

So far, we have looked at several ways of managing performance by discussion. We've considered the appropriate setting for serious discussions about performance issues, and we've reviewed some discussion topics and questions that are relevant and helpful to resolving mild behavioral and performance issues.

Now it's time to consider the more formal steps to managing performance. When discussion alone fails to bring results, or when you feel that the issue is severe enough, you need to refer to guidelines for more pointed action.

Most large companies have in place an informal progressive series of steps designed to manage performance. There are several standard ways to manage performance; such as coaching, counseling, verbal warning, written warning, and termination.

Depending on the situation, not all steps are necessary, and so use your judgment. Immediate termination may be appropriate in severe cases, whereas counseling may be acceptable in another. For the most part, whatever step or steps you decide to take to correct employee behavior make it suitable for the issue. Thoroughly investigate each issue and ensure that whatever course you prescribe; it potentially will have a positive impact on performance.

Don't formalize a performance managing process unless you intend to provide it for everyone in the company. Most companies have an 'at-will status' and creating policies relating to performance could eradicate the 'at-will status.' If you do decide to put something in writing, contact your legal counsel to ensure you are not jeopardizing your 'at-will status.'

Managers of small companies tend to wear many hats and are very busy, so they don't often have the time to coach, counsel and guide employees to higher performance. That said, the primary concern is dealing with performance issues immediately; one person's performance within a small company has a significant impact. It's critical to manage performance standards and quickly handle any performance issues.

As a manager, you are ensuring that your employees are experiencing as much success as possible. You will have a range of performance levels within your team and several different labels for employees:

- High achievers

- High performers

- Average performers

- Those who need improvement

- Those who perform below standards

There is a distinction between 'needs improvement' and 'performing below standards.' 'Needs improvement' is usually around new hires or employees who take on new responsibilities indicating they are still in the learning stage. 'Performing below standards' is geared more towards employees who have been trained and still are not performing or were performing and no longer at the level of expectation.

Even though you have performance standards, each employee is different in their approach to their responsibilities. You can't manage each employee the same way. You need to tailor your expectations of your staff by responding to the business requirements and the abilities of individuals.

> **Quick Point**
>
> When you develop appropriate performance expectations for each employee, create appropriate recognition points for each of them. Take the time to recognize performance that meets your expectations and performance that exceeds.

Here are some fundamental processes that occur in building a high-performance team:

Employment at Will

Most companies in the United States employ people "at will." Companies choose who they hire, and workers effectively decide to work at the company. The employee has the right to resign at any time for any reason, and the company has the right to terminate employment at any time, with or without cause.

At-will employment is an interesting arrangement. Both the employer and the employee recognize that the status quo depends on both parties, being satisfied with the arrangement. The at-will agreement means that neither the employee nor the employer is likely to be complacent and the relationship is potentially a positive one.

Companies are more aware of workers' needs and preferences as a means of optimizing performance, just as employees remain aware of the employer's specific needs and preferences as a means of maximizing executive-level satisfaction with their performance.

In situations where you believe it is appropriate, as the manager, you may provide employees with notice that there is a problem with their performance or conduct, thus giving them an opportunity to meet the expectations of the position. Giving your current employee time to review their actions and improve is less costly than recruiting someone new for a position.

However, providing them with notice that their performance or conduct needs to improve does not change the fact that the company is an "at-will" employer. It's important not to guarantee permanent employment to an employee. For example, telling them if they improve their performance, they will have a job. Protect the "at will" employment status by never making employment promises.

As you review this guide, it does not recommend a formal discipline process. When there is a performance or conduct issue, it may benefit both the company and the employee to discuss the problems and give time for the employee to elevate their performance or change their behaviors, though this is at the company's discretion.

If you want to maintain the company's at-will status, don't include in any documentation that you provided the employee information on a structured disciplinary process. Obviously, if the company has special contracts with employees, you must follow the formal process and procedures that the contract prescribes.

Coaching

What is coaching? It is inspiring your team to perform at expected levels by personalizing training to each on the team as well as creating productive work environments for each person to perform at their highest level.

Coaching is a two-way conversation!

Coaching is a distinct approach that focuses on a respectful relationship with employees that embraces their potential and supports their maximum performance through consistent feedback, which allows the employee to adjust their performance. Clear and consistent feedback would focus on performance as well as behaviors.

The key to effective coaching is communication. If you are not providing employees with constant and immediate feedback on the particular behavior or to recognize performance you want them to continue, you lose the value of coaching.

Managers may naturally use coaching with new hires and when an employee takes on new responsibilities. A manager stays focused on correcting performance or behaviors early on when the employee is open to correction. Coaching is an ongoing 1:1 check-in to ensure the employee feels comfortable with his or her responsibilities and can ask questions.

Coaching is the most important and most effective method for performance improvement and is an excellent way to turn a negative into a positive. In the role of coach, a manager can openly discuss an issue with their employee, investigate the situation thoroughly, and provide the employee with support to help them correct the problem.

Coaching is about communication. Effective coaching improves employee performance by clearly identifying the problem, explaining to the employee why he or she needs to resolve the problem, and demonstrating that you are there as a support system. When you coach effectively, you acknowledge to the employee that you value them and are interested in helping them in their effort to overcome the performance or behavioral issue.

This process of communication between the manager and employee is designed to assure the employee understands the job duties, performance expectations, and rules of conduct in the workplace. Today's market is competitive, and as a manager, you need to ensure that your staff knows how to do their job. If you spend time coaching your employees, odds are they will do things right the first time.

Reacting vs. Responding

Managers typically focus on performance or behaviors that either enhance or hinder performance with each person on their team. How a manager goes about ensuring that employees meet their responsibilities make a difference between an employee responding or reacting to the manager.

Reacting

An employee who reacts to a discussion with his or her manager is defensive and will not hear the message and will have an adverse reaction to the manager. Whenever anyone reacts, including the manager, it's a quick reaction without much thought and creates negativity in the communication. There is no time to think about the best solution; rather the reaction is laden with emotions.

If either you or your employee reacts on a consistent basis, this could make the situation worse and increase performance issues. Reduced trust diminishes communication.

Reactions are normal responses to stressful situations, and most people need to learn how to reframe their behaviors to build strong mutual communication between others.

When a manager decides to observe his/her behavior and uses that awareness to step back and not react to their employees, this will increase trust with others. Reactions are based on experience or future concerns and not focused on the present situation. Mindfulness practice helps individuals become aware of their thoughts and allows thoughts to pass, which increases the manager's ability to respond instead of reacting.

Responding

A manager who responds to the employees sets the tone for an employee to be in a responsive mode, thus allowing the manager and employee to have a fruitful discussion around the change in performance. This type of interaction leaves space for thinking, discussing, and reaching potentially productive solutions.

Responding allows both a manager and employee the ability to find solutions to the issue.

It's important as a manager that you lead your staff in the skill of responding vs. reacting. If you tend to react, one way to learn to build your "responding muscles" is to try mindfulness practice and pause so you can pay close attention to your reaction as well as the employees' reactions.

When you pause, take a breath, and use the space between stimulus and response wisely, so you relax and are more open to communicating respect for both you and your employee.

When you breathe deeply and become mindful of your reaction, you will see the reaction diminish, providing greater clarity for the right response to the situation.

Mindful management sets the tone for your team members, showing that you are available to listen and work with them to find decisions that create strong and respectful working partnerships.

Quick Point

Make a contract with your employees to commit to finding ways to reduce reactions and increase responses that respect everyone involved. This commitment is also good between manager/employee and between team members.

Key coaching skills

Observation

Observation skills are necessary when managing employees. A manager will watch to see if an employee needs adjustment or recognition around their performance or behaviors. Both aspects are important in coaching an employee for continuous improvement or motivation to maintain their high level of performance.

How does a manager observe performance?

- What skills or attributes are essential for the position? Knowing what is important helps to monitor performance against expectations.

- You may be able to correct or recognize performance immediately or update your notes on the employee, and when you have a 1:1 you can address either correction or recognition.

- Observe how the employee's workspace is set up and whether it supports their performance.

- If you can't observe the employee's actions directly, the results will indicate the level of performance. Take time to discuss with the employee what he or she did, how they decided to do the work, and how he or she feels about his or her performance.

- Be aware of their body language. Some employees are more open to discussing their performance while others become defensive. No matter how great you are in treating each person on your team with respect, employees have their own internal beliefs that surface in discussions. If you notice they are closing and not available to hear, ask them what they need to feel more comfortable with the discussion. Let them know that this is a discussion around how you can best support them in their work responsibilities.

Quick Point

Performance is the employee's responsibility, though he or she needs training and a manager's input on how to be most productive.

Listening

As mentioned before, when a manager can effectively listen to his or her employees, he or she will see the performance and engagement levels of team members increase significantly. Everyone looks to be heard, including you. Employees listen better when they feel their manager is attentive to them. As a manager, you can lead the way in this area and extend yourself so that the employees know you are present with them. They will learn from you.

Manager's Behaviors

A manager has a good chance of getting the employee to change his or her performance or behavior if they are both in agreement. Performance or behavior issues are the employee's problems. Having said that, you could be the cause of it, so you may need to own up to how you are impacting the employee's performance.

Building Trust

A manager needs to be aware of continuously building trust with each team member. Why is trust so important? An employee who trusts their manager is open to change, feels respected, and goes the extra mile to keep their performance and engagement high.

The manager builds trust with day-to-day interactions with the team members. You can't maximize an employee's performance and potential without a foundation of trust.

Motivation

They say it's hard to motivate an employee if they don't have an interest, are not competent in the work, or have a low threshold to work hard. Motivation comes from within an employee, though a manager can easily demotivate an employee who was initially motivated.

Here are some ideas to work with an employee's inner motivation:

- Provide a clear vision around expectations and how he or she fits into the project or success of the company.

- Find out what his or her strengths are and what excites them.

- Find out what he or she values, and do your best to create work or lifestyle that supports those values.

- Set small goals where he or she can be successful, and provide regular recognition.

- Create development opportunities for growth.

- Communicate and be transparent, so you build trust with each employee.

Feedback

Continuous feedback on an employee's performance, whether the improvement is needed or recognition of a job well done, is essential. Employees can't read your mind. Rather, you need to be mindful of their performance and let them know how they are doing. Consistent feedback fine tunes and increases performance levels. If you wait too long, then the employee doesn't know whether he or she is doing well. It's always about clear, concise, and consistent communication.

Coaching usually takes the form of verbal discussions, though you can provide written examples as guides in your discussions.

You might use coaching in the following instances:

- With new employee

- To teach a new skill

- When an employee is taking on a project that is particularly complicated

- After the first display of a mild inappropriate behavior or performance issue

Keep notes of your coaching. Refer to them when preparing employee evaluations or when counseling an employee who requires performance improvement.

Remember: your coaching helps build an effective team, one that participates in the growth of your business; with the right encouragement, every one of your employees will support your efforts to meet business objectives.

When addressing performance or behavioral issues, keep in mind that it's your role to guide your staff towards higher performance, and use your coaching skills to help your employees create solutions for their performance.

Quick Point

Do you communicate clearly to your staff the performance standards you expect from each of them? Provide them with both positive and constructive feedback.

Counseling

When you notice there's a problem with the employee's performance or conduct in the workplace, and you have already tried coaching with the employee in question, counseling is the logical second step. To effectively counsel, it's important to set time aside to privately and respectfully inform the employee about the problem, discuss how it can be solved, and, if appropriate, identify the support mechanisms the company has available to assist in resolving the problem (i.e., mentoring, training).

During a counseling session, make sure your employee is aware of the problem, and impress upon them the importance and necessity of correcting it. Most employees will respond positively to this meeting and will go on to remedy the problem, but if the problem continues, you may need to initiate disciplinary action.

Retain a written record of counseling, including the date, the subjects discussed, the expectations communicated to the employee, and the proposed method for monitoring the employee's performance. (*See Attachment A - Sample Counseling Template*).

Disciplinary Process

<u>Verbal warning</u>

If, after counseling, the employee fails to solve the performance issue or fails to bring their conduct to an acceptable level, the next step is to issue a verbal warning. The purpose of this step is to clarify the direction for necessary and successful correction of the problem.

Give a verbal warning in a private office. Try to create a positive environment so that the employee will be receptive to the discussion. Focus on the job performance (*e.g.,* "you failed to meet your targeted sales quota") and not the person (*e.g.,* "you don't seem to have what it takes to be a salesperson").

As a model for discussion with employees, open the meeting describing the performance issues(s) that need their focus. Be specific about what, where, when, and how the performance issue(s) seem to have arisen. After explaining the issue to the employee, give them time to provide feedback. During the meeting, if appropriate, you may identify support mechanisms (mentoring or training).

At the end of the discussion, summarize and review the important points. State and document the recommended action plan and the period for completion. Schedule a follow-up date. After the meeting, monitor the employee's performance against the expectations. (*See Attachment "B" - Sample Letter to File for Verbal Warning*)

Written Warning

If a verbal warning is not successful in turning the situation around or if the situation is sufficiently serious, it may be necessary to issue a written warning and place a copy of the documentation in the employee's file.

To make a written warning useful, you need to meet with the employee, present them with the letter, listen to their responses, specify the next steps, and have the employee sign the document which indicates they are aware that their level of performance or behavior requires change. (*See Attachment C - Performance Improvement Plan Document.*)

Suspension Pending Investigation

There are situations when the employee must be removed from the workplace immediately, and a formal investigation conducted. Cases requiring this type of action include theft, disorderly conduct, or threatening behavior to other employees. *(See Serious Employee Work Issues above)*.

The very first step when dealing with serious employee issues is to check with your legal counsel. Pending the results of an investigation, suspension of the employee is the first action.

A suspension occurs with the understanding that a final decision happens after an investigation of the employee's infraction. If there is no cause for disciplinary action, the employee will receive pay for regular earnings lost during the suspension.

Work with your Human Resources department or legal counsel around suspensions.

Time Frames

Timing is always critical in the disciplinary process. What can you do if an employee, after coaching, counseling, or a verbal warning, is still not able to correct their performance or conduct in the workplace?

No set time must elapse between the performance improvement steps. Before the process begins, the manager must decide what an appropriate time frame for resolving the performance issue or conduct is. Allow enough time for the employee to correct the problem. Maybe a couple of days, a week, a month, or several months, depending upon the nature of the problem. The manager explains to the employee the expected timeframe for improvement.

In situations where the employee can resolve the problem quickly, such as attendance problems or sloppy work, communicate your expectation that he or she immediately achieves and maintains acceptable performance standards to avoid further disciplinary action. In situations where the employee needs to develop a skill or learn a procedure, it may be appropriate to follow up with a date farther out (*e.g.,* 30-60 days).

Monitor the employee's progress and document throughout this period. Once the skill is learned or a certain level of proficiency attained, it is essential to communicate the expectation they maintain this level of performance.

If the employee modifies his or her performance to meet acceptable standards, then a follow-up document needs to be created stating that the employee is now meeting the performance standards as outlined in his or her performance plan.

What are Performance Improvement Plans?

A Performance Improvement Plan (PIP) is a manager's plan of action for dealing with inappropriate behavior and performance issues, but it is slightly more than a list of ways to solve a performance or behavioral issue.

Before a manager can implement a performance plan for the company, he or she must be sure to have a definite idea about what the company's performance objectives are. As the manager, you need to decide the general and specific goals of their business. You also need to assess how each of your employees needs to contribute to achieving business goals.

You can think about the company's goals in some ways:

- o What are the company's long-term and short-term goals?

- o If you have different departments in the company, what are the different department goals?

- o How do you plan to divide general responsibilities?

o Will you delegate some of your responsibilities?

o What are the specific performance goals for each of your employees?

o How will you review the company's performance and assess the performance of your staff?

o How often will you communicate with your employees regarding their performance and attainment?

When you have a clear idea of expectations for behavior and performance, share this information with the employees.

One of the most fundamental elements of a healthy work environment is all-around respect. As a manager, treat your employees and colleagues with respect and set an example for the office. Of course, one of the ways to instill respect is treating everyone fairly. Before you can take disciplinary action against any employee, even if all you suggest for them is counseling, you have to make sure that all of your employees are aware of expected behavior and performance levels.

There are some ways to ensure that your employees have information around expectations. For example, you can establish expectations of your employees in their contracts. You can provide general office guidelines for behavior and make those guidelines available to everyone in your office.

A performance plan is also a set of guidelines; not, in most cases, a formal set policy for discipline. Instead, a performance plan is designed to help employees who have fallen short of expectations by providing them with information and assistance to correct the problem.

Company Values

As a manager, you are responsible for managing the performance standards of your staff. You are also responsible for establishing, formally or otherwise, the intrinsic values of the company.

Consider these questions:

- o What are the company's core values?
- o How do you promote the values through your actions with your staff?

If the company does not have stated values that drive the day-to-day success, establish core values that you as a manager are committed to when interacting with your staff.

The following are some basic and satisfactory values you can promote with your team. Consider how well your employees implement each of these values and think about how you can promote these values in the work environment.

Accountability

When your team values accountability, everyone can be counted on to meet obligations or take responsibility for his or her mistakes. Your team will adhere to company policies and procedures such as goal setting, purchasing and expense reports, time reporting and travel plans. You may also implement programs so that your employees can take part in establishing company policies and procedures that are the most effective. Encourage your employees to measure their performance and, most importantly, help them to work as a team to achieve common goals.

Customer Commitment

Customer commitment involves anticipating internal and external customer needs and taking actions to meet them. When the company values customer commitment, your employees search for ways to increase customer satisfaction. Also look to develop strong influencing skills in your employees, such as the ability to sell products, services, or concepts to customers inside and outside the company.

Innovation and Creativity

When you and your employees generate new and unique ideas to enhance methods, products, or quality or cost improvements, the company is demonstrating innovation and creativity. Be open to new ideas and able to adjust quickly to changing priorities and unexpected demands. Your employees champion new initiatives and breakthrough solutions and use creative thinking to approach problems.

Open Communication

Open communication promotes and maintains a positive work atmosphere. It discourages "us versus them" thinking. It demonstrates respect for others' points of view. Open communication encourages others to express contrary views. It treats customers and co-workers with dignity and respect. It uses diplomacy and tact and is cool under pressure. It conveys necessary information to others. Open communication includes good written, verbal, and presentation skills. It can get a message across that has the desired effect. It genuinely listens to others.

Productivity

Valuing productivity means that you, as the manager, make it enjoyable for your employees to work hard and be energetic about new challenges. Your employees need to work independently, be proactive self-starters, able to determine the next steps and do it without being told. Encourage your staff to use time effectively for planning, organizing, and executing work. Support them in setting priorities appropriately and eliminate roadblocks to productivity. You, as the manager, need to know how to get things done in a complex multi-level, matrix organization. Encourage your employees to maintain good attendance and punctuality.

Quality

When it comes to assessing quality, are your employees dedicated to delivering the highest quality results? Do they accurately and thoroughly complete assignments, show attention to detail, and demonstrate a commitment to providing high-quality products and services to customers and co-workers. When the company values quality, encourage your employees to seek opportunities to do things better. Work to create a productive environment that leads to the most efficient work process possible.

Respect

Without your staff, you can't meet your business objectives. To succeed at motivating your team, you will need to communicate with them respectfully. You may be in a meeting with your team and not agree with someone's ideas. Finding the right way to communicate is critical to your success as a manager. If you value the input of your employees and respect them as contributors, you need to communicate this. Don't make your greatest resource – your staff – afraid to speak up.

Let your staff know you respect them. Assume each person wants to respect as you would, and you may find them willing to go the extra mile for you. Your staff will imitate your behavior, and it will affect theirs. Focus on creating a respectful workplace in which everyone feels their contributions are valued.

Deal with Employee Complaints

Take the time to listen to an employee's point of view when there is a problem with his or her behavior or performance. Consider whether you are responsible for the issue the employee is experiencing.

When an employee presents a problem, address the issue quickly. The performance will suffer when employees have complaints. Some of the most common problems for employees are:

- co-workers
- working conditions

- supervisory support
- job security
- career development
- money

If you can find the time to discuss such matters with your staff, your employees will be more productive. An active manager makes time to listen carefully to the employee's concerns.

Of course, for employees who choose "complaining" as their primary communication with you, create clear boundaries with them. You can tell them, "I'm here to listen for 5 minutes, and it would be great if you would state what you need as well as potential solutions. Then we can work together to come up with an appropriate solution." Make your expectations clear to your staff.

> **Quick Point**
>
> Listen to your staff's issues – establish that you expect them to come prepared with some solutions to their problems. This way they are part of the solution and are more invested in their performance.

When are Performance Plans used?

Most employees need only basic training and information to be productive. Particularly in at-will employment situations, it is in the best interest of the employee to behave respectfully to colleagues and customers. Performing at their best is also seen to be advantageous as well, for the same obvious reasons. That said, there are times when personal issues can make someone unhappy and unstable at work. Any employee who is tired and under pressure creates a recipe for behavioral and performance issues. You and your employees are only human, after all.

As a manager, however, it's your job to work with an employee whose performance or conduct is lacking on a given occasion. Negativity in the workplace is bad for business; you need to handle the situation efficiently and help your employees understand the significance of their actions.

When appropriate, you can refer to your performance plan to help an employee when the behavior has fallen short of expectations. Ensure that your employees are aware of expected behavior; if they knowingly fall short of expectations, it's the time to refer to your performance plan and reinforce the importance of proper behavior and attitude in the workplace.

The same happens when an employee's performance has fallen short. So long as they are aware of expectation, you are right to establish some form of corrective action when they fall short (we'll look at the different types of action later).

The key to effective discipline in the workplace is to remember its objective. The purpose of discipline is always performance improvement, not punishment.

This guide will address ways to handle employee issues: poor work performance, personal conduct, or attendance. This guide describes the essential elements of a performance plan and is intended to assist you in your role as manager. It is designed to help you determine when disciplinary action is necessary, what level of discipline is appropriate, and how to administer the appropriate discipline.

This guide will help you create a productive work environment, but it does not address the "grievance" process. The contract describes the process between the employee and employer. The guide does not deal with the most serious employee issues that require immediate action, such as violent behavior (*See "Serious Employee Work Issues"*).

Quick Point

Performance plans focus on improvement -- helping the employee become better at what they do. As a manager, you may become frustrated with the performance of the employee, and it's important to recognize this is not a process for punishment or to release your frustration, but rather a vehicle for building stronger performance levels.

Serious Employee Work Issues

Not all employee work issues are the same. The following is a list of situations that demand immediate attention and response, and have either your human resources department or legal counsel lead the investigation.

- Sexual harassment

- Drug or alcohol abuse

- Breaking a company rule or engaging in unacceptable conduct

- Insubordination

- Action dangerous to self or others

- Possession of prohibited substance

- Illegal activity on premises

- Violation of the non-solicitation policy

- Another issue that is being impacted by employee's actions

Performance-Based Issues

Do you have employees who...?

- Are chronically late or absent?

- Fail to follow procedures?

- Engage in inappropriate behavior?

- Fail to meet job expectations?

These are common performance-based issues that all managers are expected to handle.

Whenever you are addressing a concern or a particular problem with an employee, it is important that you have all of the facts. Review the details and include the employee's explanation before moving forward on a disciplinary action.

It is *critical* that in your role as a manager that you are fair, objective, and respectful, holding all employees within your department to the same standards of performance or behavior. Think about how you want to be treated and do the same for them.

Questions to Ask Around a Performance Problem

- Is the substandard performance a pattern or a recent development? If recent, probe into the reasons for the current level of performance. If the issue is personal, recommend that the employee contact your Human Resources representative for possible resources to help them with their problem. If you don't have an HR

Department, ask the employee what he or she needs to boost his or her performance during this challenging time. If the solution is doable for you, this is the perfect time to build goodwill with your employees by showing them that you are willing to work with them.

- Have similar events occurred in the past? Has the employee been counseled previously on the issue in question or on a same problem?

- Does the employee have the necessary skills, knowledge, abilities, and temperament to do the job?

- Has the employee received adequate training, guidance, and feedback?

- Has there been a change in the workload volume, increase in stress, staffing shortages, or any other changes that may be impacting performance for this employee?

- Are system barriers beyond the employee's control contributing to the performance problems?

- Does the employee have the proper tools, equipment, support, and work environment?

- Is this an "attitude" issue?

"Attitude" Issue

An employee with an attitude problem can be a challenge for a manager. A "bad attitude" can poison the work environment, leading to a decrease in morale and productivity. Some conduct may rise to the level of insubordination, resulting in termination; such as refusal to perform a directive from their manager. Lesser conduct, such as sighing, rolling their eyeballs, or making a negative response to a manager's request needed not be tolerated but dealt with quickly.

To stop undesirable behavior, schedule a face-to-face private meeting to explain how the employee's actions are perceived and what you would like to see changed.

Open the discussion by describing the complaints in general terms. The next step is to ask about the reason for the negative behavior. Is there a personal issue? Does the employee have a problem with someone or a work-related issue? Be open to discussing any such problems before moving on.

Once you've established what's going on with the employee and he or she knows how the behavior is perceived, the next step is for you to explain why poor attitude needs their attention; why it's bad for business.

When all this is clear, you can move on to discussing your course of action. Explain that the situation requires change of behavior, establish a time frame for the change to take place, and let them know that there will be follow-up on the problem to ensure it is solved. If you are recommending coaching, counseling, or any other formal action, explain your reasoning to the employee as a means of promoting a sense of fairness.

> **Quick Point**
>
> When discussing the problem with your employee,
> avoid stating "you need to improve your attitude."
> This statement is too vague and does not give the
> necessary feedback to the employee on their
> behavior. Instead, focus on the behavior itself, *i.e.*,
> the tone of voice, the use of inappropriate
> gestures, the resistance to accepting direction, the
> negative response, etc.

Termination

Again, most companies are under an "at will"
provision, which means they can terminate anyone
at any time. Because managers don't want to lose
potentially good people, they are willing to
support an employee via performance
improvement plans. Normally termination is the

last step of a disciplinary process with an employee.

Serious work issues such sexual harassment, breaking a company policy, theft, or drug or alcohol abuse on the premises are all reasons for possible immediate termination.

I would recommend consulting all termination decisions with Human Resources (if available) and/or legal counsel. The reason this is important is to ensure that the termination is not occurring due to discrimination or sexual harassment.

If, after a careful review, termination is deemed appropriate, you, as the manager, and Human Resources plan the termination meeting. You can create the final document stating the reasons for the termination, indicating what performance or behavior issues were problematic and how they were not corrected. Always tell the employee the truth about the causes of the action. It is critical that you maintain confidentiality and document everything stated at the termination meeting. Treat the employee with respect throughout the process.

In the decision-making course, recognize that termination, though uncomfortable, is a viable solution when handled respectfully. If an employee can't do the work and is stressed, it is the right decision to let him, or her find another opportunity to excel, as well as provide the right work environment where all employees are performing at acceptable levels.

In preparing & planning for the termination, the manager will:

- Create the final separation document, setting forth the reason(s) for termination of employment.

- Review the employee's personnel file, records of prior counseling, verbal, and/or written warnings, and any other pertinent documentation with Human Resources.

- Decide when and where to hold the termination meeting. Select a secluded location, away from view by other employees. The best time for the meeting is at the end of the day to minimize interaction with co-workers. The middle of the week is preferable to a Friday when the employee will have the weekend ahead to brood over the termination.

- Anticipate and be prepared for the employee's reaction to the termination - are there security issues?

- Notify HR/Help Desk to secure the computer and telephone systems, security badges, passwords, keycards, and other company property. Make sure you have an Exit Document in place so that you can forward to HR/Help Desk.

- Plan for the employee to get personal files off their computer, as well as removing personal items from the work area.

- Create a list of all people who will be affected by this termination and decide where the work is to go after the person leaves.

- Plan the message for notifying clients and employees who work with the impacted employee. Coordinate all messaging with Human Resources and legal counsel.

In conducting the termination:

- Arrange for a representative from Human Resources to be present. If that is not possible, have another manager or supervisor present.

- Stay focused on communicating the facts of the decision – do not let the discussion become personal. Focus on the issue and not on the person.

- Be ready for the employee's reaction and let him or her vent a little completion of the termination. Only allow about 5 minutes before helping him, or she realizes that this is a termination.

- Do not allow for negotiation; emphasize that the decision is final.

- Advise co-workers that the employee no longer works for the company. Coordinate with Human Resources and legal counsel.

- Advise supervisors and co-workers what the "company statement" will be for clients or others calling for the employee. (Advise them to direct all further inquiries to Human Resources or one individual in your organization who knows how to respond to outside questions.)

- Communicate to all parties affected by this termination and let them know who will be responsible for the work.

- Document the termination meeting and place all documentation in the employee's file.

Summary

This guide is intended to support you in the development of your employees. Managers are responsible for creating an environment that ensures retention of the best and the brightest. In following these basic performance guidelines, you can develop a strong team to support your business needs. Keep in mind what is important:

- Be consistent and fair in your treatment of all employees

- Support self-esteem

- Emphasize employee responsibility

- Set accountability standards

- Provide timely and specific feedback

- Document, document, document

- Consult with your HR partner or legal counsel

Attachments

Attachment "A" - Sample Counseling Template

Employee Name:

Title:

Date:

Follow Up Date:

Issues Discussed:

Expectations Communicated:

Potential Solutions:

Letter to File: Verbal Warning

TO: Employee File

FROM: (Manager)

DATE:

SUBJECT: Disciplinary meeting with (employee's name)

RE: (reason for action)

A meeting was held……. (date, who attended).

At this meeting (what was discussed).

- Explain performance issue(s) (what happened, where it happened, how it happened, when it happened and who was involved)
- Employee's explanation about the problem(s)
- If appropriate, identify support mechanisms (mentoring or training)
- Create action plan

- Set up next meeting date to follow up on performance issue(s)

(Employee) was informed that this was a verbal warning and that the copy of the document is put in his/her employee file.

Cc: Employee file

Employee:

Meeting date:

Manager:

Performance Issue Being Reviewed: (Productivity, Teamwork, Quality of work, Attendance, Conduct, Other)

Give specific examples of current performance under review: (State time and date of incidents/issues and describe the problem/event in sufficient detail. Also state how this has interfered with the work environment, operations, or performance of the employee.)

Improvement Plan (Explain what the employee must do to improve performance or change behavior, as well as the timeframe for the expected performance or behavior improvement.)

Employee Acknowledgement
By my signature, below, I acknowledge the following:

- This memo has been discussed with me on the date noted.
- I have received a copy of this memo.
- I know that a copy is in my employee file.
- I understand that I may not receive an incentive payout because of my performance.
- I understand that this performance plan is not intended to be an employment contract or guarantee of continuing employment.
- I agree to follow the action plan guidelines as described in this memo, effective immediately. I understand that if I do not follow the action plan guidelines, I may be subject to further discipline, including termination from the company.

Employee Signature & Date
Supervisor's Signature & Date
Performance Plan to employee's file (date)
Follow Up Date to Evaluate Performance:
(First one is within 2 weeks, and then schedule appropriate times after the initial meeting.)
Fully meeting performance expectations (date)

Forward to Human Resources (or personal responsible for employee files)

Exiting Employee (full name):
Requested by (manager):
Date of Request:
Exit Interview Scheduled
Exit Date and Time:

Disable Network Access (default is **yes**). If **no**, please explain:
Does anyone in the department need a copy or access to the individual's email box?

Disable Voicemail Account (default is **yes**). If **no**, please explain
Does anyone in your department need a copy or access to the individual's voice mail?

Does the individual have corporate credit cards?
Does the individual have a laptop? If so, who is to get the laptop?

Normally, the manager of the department needs the data content of a laptop. The Technology Department is usually the keeper of all laptops and desktops.

Office Equipment: The Facilities Manager handles the office equipment.

Manager's Signature and Date:

About the Author

Pat Brill creates empowering coaching connections that build strong and successful managers. From sourcing to hiring to effective evaluation and connective communication strategies, Pat brings twenty years of experience directly to your management goals. After earning the highest certification possible in her field Sr. Professional of Human Resources, Pat has dedicated her life to inspiring managers to excel at their roles.

Pat's extensive work with managers has given her a unique perspective on what works for a manager's success. Combining her management, leadership, and coaching experience, Pat has broken down the key success strategies she's collected into a new series of up-to-the-minute guides for the professional manager. She believes that a successful business and productive team requires flexible, nimble, and practical, not theoretical, interpersonal management strategies.

While there has been a lot of information available to managers on business systems, what Pat finds is that managers often feel unsupported and unskilled in the "human quotient" elements—communication, connection, and other invaluable skills necessary for building a productive and proactive professional relationship.

Nowhere are these interpersonal elements more important than between a manager and his or her team! In this new series of "virtual coaching" guides, Pat takes the successful methods she's employed in her one-on-one coaching and consulting work and puts it in the palm of your hand! Here you will find the re-energizing and re-focusing strategies you need whether you are leading a start-up, an established corporate team, or anything in between.

Don't leave your success up to chance, corporate theory, or haphazard processes! Empower your management transformation to build the best systems possible with the coaching connection Pat Brill offers. To learn more about her training, "virtual coaching guides" or other services visit ManagingEmployees.net

Managing Employees Series

Current Guides

Recruiting the Best Talent
Performance Management: Coach, Counsel or
Terminate

Made in the USA
Coppell, TX
26 December 2019